POINTS OF VIEW

Is Safety More Important Than PRIVACY?

By Menna Landon

KidHaven PUBLISHING

Published in 2022 by
KidHaven Publishing, an Imprint of Greenhaven Publishing, LLC
353 3rd Avenue
Suite 255
New York, NY 10010

Designer: Deanna Paternostro
Editor: Caitie McAneney

Photo credits: Cover Africa Studio/Shutterstock.com; pp. 5,19 Jamie Grill/Getty Images; p. 7 Thomas Barwick/DigitalVision/Getty Images; p. 9 Robyn Beck/Staff/AFP/Getty Images; p. 11 Westend61/Getty Images; p. 13 Chip Somodevilla/Staff/Getty Images News/Getty Images; p. 15 (main) Fertnig/E+/Getty Images; p. 15 (inset) Thanit Weerawan/Moment/Getty Images; p. 17 (main) FG Trade/E+/Getty Images; p. 17 (inset) simonkr/E+/Getty Images; p. 21 (notepad) ESB Professional/Shutterstock.com; p. 21 (markers) Kucher Serhii/Shutterstock.com; p. 21 (photo frame) FARBAI/iStock/Thinkstock; p. 21 (inset, left) Ariel Skelley/DigitalVision/Getty Images; p. 21 (inset, middle left) Jeff Greenberg/Universal Images Group/Getty Images; p. 21 (inset, middle right) Monty Rakusen/Cultura/Getty Images; p. 21 (inset, right) Uwe Krejci/DigitalVision/Getty Images.

Library of Congress Cataloging-in-Publication Data

Names: Landon, Menna, author.
Title: Is safety more important than privacy? / Menna Landon.
Description: New York : KidHaven Publishing, [2022] | Series: Points of view | Includes bibliographical references and index.
Identifiers: LCCN 2020030797 | ISBN 9781534536593 (library binding) | ISBN 9781534536579 (paperback) | ISBN 9781534536586 (set) | ISBN 9781534536609 (ebook)
Subjects: LCSH: Crime prevention–Technological innovations–Juvenile literature. | Electronic surveillance–Juvenile literature. | Privacy, Right of–Juvenile literature. | Data protection–Juvenile literature.
Classification: LCC HV7431 .L36 2022 | DDC 364.4–dc23
LC record available at https://lccn.loc.gov/2020030797

Printed in the United States of America

CONTENTS

Private EYES

You might prefer that some things you think or feel be kept private. Maybe you keep a diary about your thoughts and feelings. Maybe you want to talk to a close friend about something, and you don't want your parents or teacher to hear.

Some people argue that privacy is a basic right. They think everyone, including kids, should be able to keep personal information, or facts, private. Other people believe that safety is more important than privacy. For example, they might think your parents should be able to read your diary to make sure you're staying safe and out of trouble.

Know the Facts!

People often argue about privacy and safety when they talk about surveillance. Surveillance is the act of watching someone or something closely, often when they don't know about it.

Privacy is the ability to keep things private, or secret. Is it more important than keeping yourself and others safe? You can form an informed, or educated, opinion about this by looking at both sides.

That's Private INFORMATION!

The issue of privacy versus safety isn't just a concern for kids. Adults worry about it too, especially when it comes to surveillance and **data** gathering. Companies gather and use personal data, such as your age, tastes, and interests, to see what you might like to buy. The government and police might use collected data to find someone who is lost or in trouble.

Some people are uncomfortable with anyone using their data. Others don't mind, as long as it keeps everyone safer. Overall, about 81 percent of Americans believe the dangers of their data being gathered outweigh any benefits.

Know the Facts!

A 2015 Pew Research Center report showed 93 percent of Americans believe being in control of who can get information about them is important.

Think about your own private data. Are you concerned about people you don't know gathering basic data, such as your age, name, and address? What about your interests and private thoughts?

Lost and FOUND

Some kids might not like it when their parents ask where they are at all times or use **GPS** tracking on their phone. Others might argue that parents are making sure their kids are in a safe place. This kind of tracking and surveillance can keep people safe. It can save them from being lost or hurt or keep them from getting in trouble.

Some people are more likely to get lost than others. For example, some people with **autism spectrum disorder** might wander from home without being prepared. GPS tracking **devices** can help caretakers and community helpers get them home safely.

Know the Facts!

If someone is lost on a hike in the wilderness, the police can contact their phone's service provider to get their GPS information. This may help them find the person quickly to get them back to safety.

GPS tracking devices can help find people who have wandered from home or are in a place that's not safe.

Always WATCHING

Some people don't like feeling watched or followed. Kids might feel they can't do anything without their parents or school finding out. Some get upset because they feel they can't go anywhere on their own. Some don't like that parents can check their bedrooms or teachers can search their lockers. It might make them feel on edge.

Similarly, some adults don't like being watched or tracked by the government or companies either. They don't like when law enforcement officials, or police, put cameras in public places. They're bothered when companies record their moves online or when smart devices "listen in."

Know the Facts!

A 2016 Pew Research Center poll found that 48 percent of parents looked through their teen children's calls and text messages.

Many kids and teens struggle with wanting more freedom. Privacy can be a big part of that freedom.

Surveillance Stops TROUBLE

Other people believe it's important for **authorities**—including parents, teachers, and police—to be able to use surveillance. That's one way they can stop trouble. For example, imagine a student is bullying a classmate on **social media**. Their teachers and other school authorities might look at their social media posts to try to stop the bullying before it gets worse.

Police sometimes use surveillance to find criminals, or people who break the law. They can track phones to find criminals. They can also use surveillance cameras—and even police robots—to record images of possible criminals to make it easier to find them.

Know the Facts!

In 2019, Facebook gathered more than 200,000 "digital fingerprints" from **terrorist** images and messages. Facebook shared this data with other social media companies so they could look out for harmful content from those people.

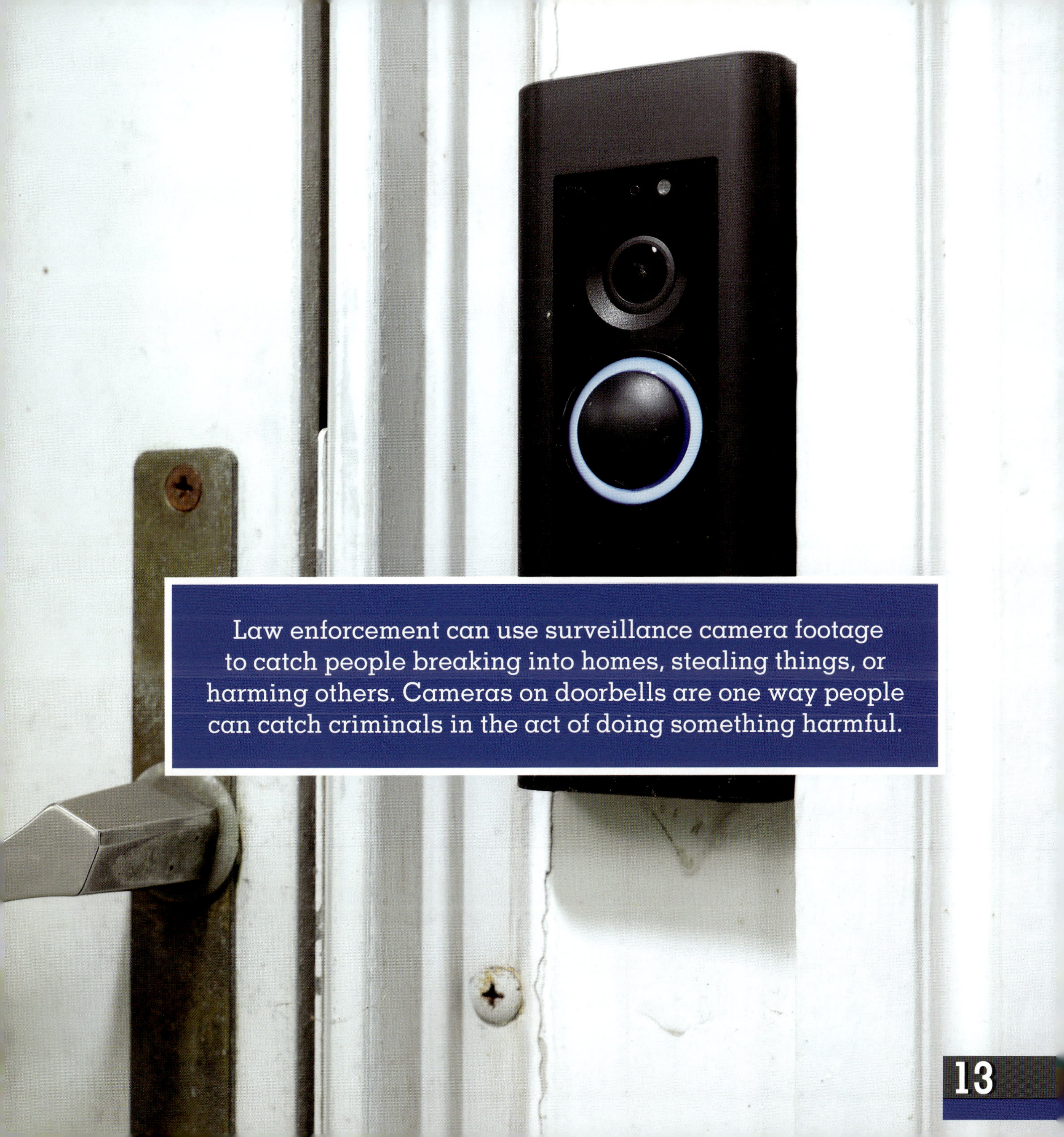

Law enforcement can use surveillance camera footage to catch people breaking into homes, stealing things, or harming others. Cameras on doorbells are one way people can catch criminals in the act of doing something harmful.

A Basic RIGHT

Some people see privacy as a basic right for everyone. They think they should be able to say, do, or write what they want without others finding it or using it against them.

Some people think surveillance will be used to keep them from using their other basic rights, such as freedom of speech or freedom to **protest**. Some people worry that police can keep track of people taking part in protests through surveillance. This could keep people from protesting at all. In a similar example, a young person might be afraid to express their true opinions in a journal if they know their teacher will read it.

Know the Facts!

The Bill of Rights spells out the basic rights of all U.S. citizens. These include freedom of speech, religion, and the press, as well as the right to peacefully protest.

Some kids feel that parents, teachers, and other adults are watching them all the time. Some adults feel this way about the government. They think the government is watching their every move.

Just CHECKING!

Many kids and teens get upset when parents and teachers search their **property** in their bedrooms or lockers or even check their online accounts. Many adults argue that they're just checking to make sure there's nothing harmful there.

Have you ever gone to a concert or gone on a plane? If so, you've had to go through a **security** checkpoint. Security agents check to make sure you have nothing harmful. They check anything you carry on your body. Some people might feel like security agents aren't respecting their privacy. However, others argue that this keeps everyone safe from harmful objects, such as **weapons**.

Know the Facts!

Security at airports got stronger after terrorist attacks on September 11, 2001, killed thousands of Americans. Some people believe the increased security has made it safer to fly.

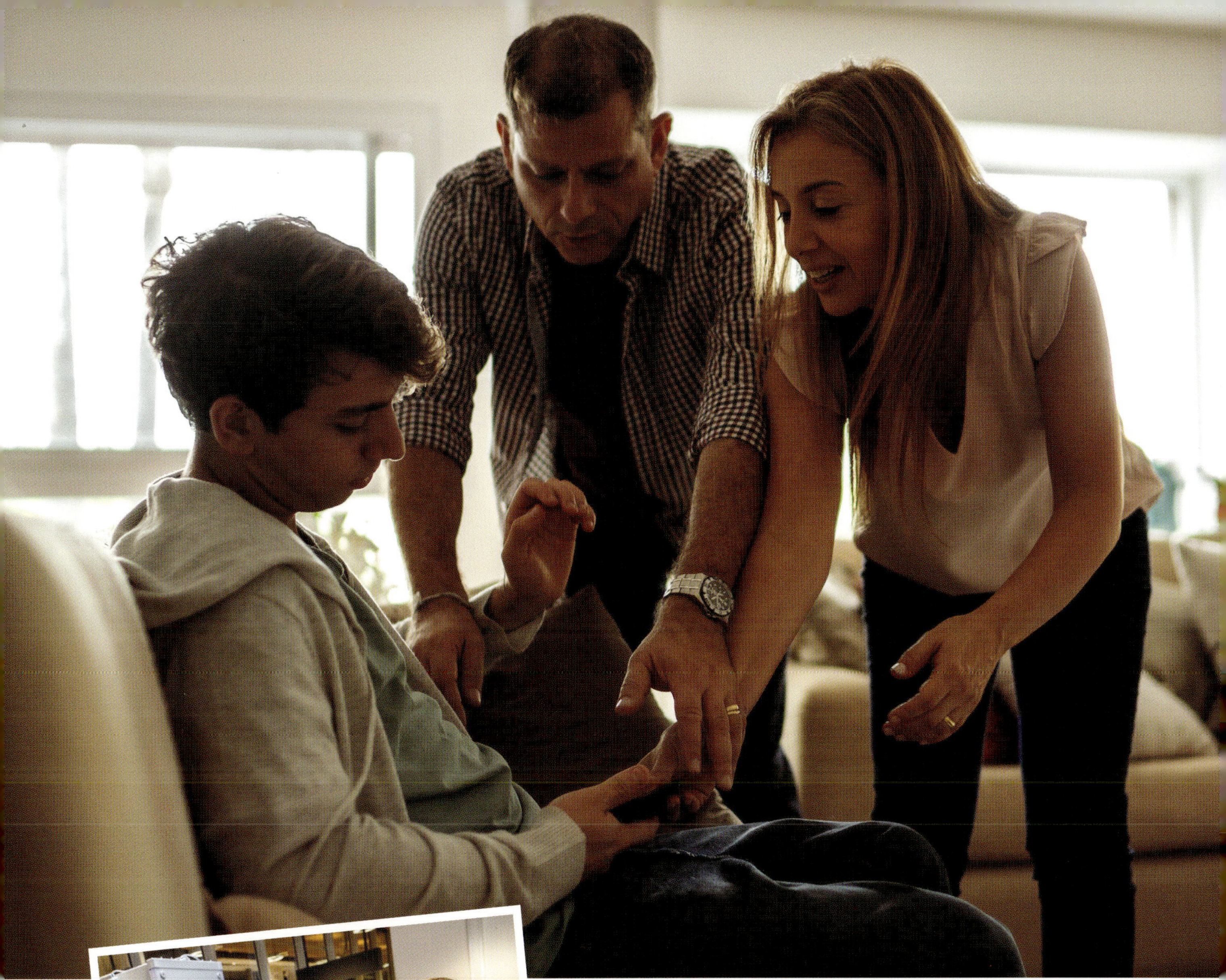

Adults checking a teenager's phone and security agents checking bags at an airport all believe they're doing what needs to be done to keep people safe.

Just TRUST

As kids grow older, they might want more privacy—and more trust—from their parents. Some parents check up on the websites their child uses or search their room. That makes some kids feel like there's no trust between them. Some feel they have no control over their personal space or social lives.

Some parents follow their kids on social media or check their profiles regularly. They might also ask for their passwords for gaming systems and social media accounts. They might read text messages or listen to phone calls. Some kids and teens argue this breaks down trust between them.

Know the Facts!

A Pew Research poll found that in 2016, 61 percent of parents checked the websites their teen used and 60 percent checked their teen's social media profiles.

Some parents use parental controls to keep their kids and teens from visiting certain websites.

Finding a COMPROMISE

Some people want the ability to keep their data, thoughts, and interests private. They don't like when others keep track of their location, check their property, or know their passwords.

Others believe the only way to keep people safe is to keep track of what they do and where they go. They think people need surveillance to stay out of trouble and away from harm. This issue affects young people, but adults also worry, especially when it comes to police and government surveillance. What do you think? Is there a good **compromise** between privacy and safety?

Know the Facts!

More than half of American children own a smartphone by age 11. Smartphones allow people to use the internet.

Is safety more important than privacy?

YES

- Tracking people can keep them safe and can help find them if they're lost.
- Surveillance can stop bullying and other harmful actions.
- Surveillance can keep people safer by catching criminals.
- Checking a person's property can keep them and others safe from harmful objects such as weapons.

NO

- People should have control over their personal data, as well as the things they say and write.
- People should be able to do what they want without surveillance.
- Privacy is a right, and taking it away could lead to other rights being taken away.
- Overstepping privacy boundaries breaks down trust.

What's more important to you—privacy or safety? Your experiences, or life events, can also inform your argument.

GLOSSARY

authority: A person who has power or responsibility over someone else.

autism spectrum disorder: One of any of a group of disorders in which a person may have trouble communicating, sharing knowledge and feelings, or being social with others.

compromise: A way of two sides reaching agreement in which each gives up something.

data: Facts and figures.

device: A tool used for a certain purpose.

GPS: A navigating system that uses satellite signals to tell the user where they are and direct them to a destination.

property: Something that someone owns.

protest: To speak out strongly against something. Also, an event at which people speak out about something.

security: Having to do with the quality of being safe from danger.

social media: A collection of websites and applications, or apps, that allow users to interact with each other and create online communities.

terrorist: Having to do with using violence and fear to challenge an authority.

weapon: Something used to hurt someone.

For More INFORMATION

WEBSITES

Know Your Rights: Students' Rights
www.aclu.org/know-your-rights/students-rights/
Learn more about your rights in school.

Online Safety
kidshealth.org/en/kids/online-id.html
Learn some ways to stay safe and keep your information as private as possible online.

BOOKS

Barcella, Laura. *Know Your Rights: A Modern Kid's Guide to the American Constitution*. New York, NY: Sterling Children's Books, 2018.

Noll, Elizabeth. *Police Robots (World of Robots)*. Minneapolis, MN: Bellwether Media, 2018.

Schuette, Sarah L. *Online Safety*. Mankato, MN: Capstone Press, 2020.

Publisher's note to educators and parents: Our editors have carefully reviewed these websites to ensure that they are suitable for students. Many websites change frequently, however, and we cannot guarantee that a site's future contents will continue to meet our high standards of quality and educational value. Be advised that students should be closely supervised whenever they access the Internet.

INDEX